Plath's Oven

Aadesh Bhangre

BookLeaf Publishing

Presentation by *BookLeaf Publishing*

Web: www.bookleafpub.com

E-mail: info@bookleafpub.com

ISBN: 978-93-95621-24-3

First edition 2022

DEDICATION

To the push that Sylvia Plath gave me into the abyss of her mind. Some depths have been covered. A lot is left to unearth. One thing we know for sure is that there is no bottom to this pit.

Ashes Of The Phoenix

The phoenix takes nine days to rise from the
ashes
What would happen if all the winds
Took those ashes away?

Will they spread some spark across the world?
Or will they keep floating as particles of dust?

Would it then matter that the winds your breathe
Are that of a mortal creature?

Or will it just be another filth of the earth?

Heaven Is A Place On Earth

The mountains don't bleed
They stay still
The rivers don't weep
They keep flowing

And the children of the valley,
They don't say a word
Their silences scream though
And get muffled under the patriotic cry

It doesn't matter
If they belong to this country
Or the one across the border
Since the lines are drawn with their blood

For they are just innocent cattle
Waiting to be slaughtered
They will be milked for their bounties
Then be labelled as traitors

Their pain is for the greater good
But what good does it do to anyone
Watching their mothers defiled
Watching their fathers die

Is this what's a democracy?
That sounds more like a mockery
Daughters of the land of heaven
Standing on the world's largest grave

These are the hollow-eyed girls
From a place called Jannat
They say heaven is a place on earth
But isn't it also a place for the dead?

Name

I will write my name when
It becomes a name
Worthy of being written

I will write my name when
It becomes a name
That is worth remembering

And I will write my name when
When the name starts to mean
Something to someone

But most importantly
I will write my name when
It means something to me

Melancholy's Babies

What do you know about comfort?
For nothing comforts like a coffin

You say your heart is heavy,
Can it be bulkier than Virginia's coat?

There is a pill for every problem
Hemingway's was loaded in a gun

Hang in there, David Wallace
Cuz we are coming too

Let's take that road trip Toole took
With a longer garden hose though

Or let's just go back to sleep again
But sleep in Plath's oven this time

Melancholy's babies that we are
We'll make snow angels in heaven

Only Tree In A Forest

How does it feel to be
strangled by your own roots?
Stunted by your own shoots?

Every drop of water feels like poison
And every fruit is forbidden

Where all the flowers are dark
Not a single merry bird on bark

You are your own parasite
Leeching yourself from inside

The sun doesn't shine
And the birds don't sing
And no, winds don't sway

Floods won't take you away
and no woodcutters don't care

You'll just be hanging out there
Till you rot from within
And then wither away

Welcome To The Closet
(With Pride)

And there comes down the giant rainbow heart
Folded from the centre
It breaks into half
But it doesn't hurt
Our hearts have been broken before
They still do every now and then

The cracks in the cardboard spine
The creaking of the candy sticks
Somehow sounds deafening
But it doesn't hurt
We have screamed louder
And silenced almost every time

The heart wasn't that heavy
Not when it was installed
Yet this time it seemed so

So heavy, it had to be dragged
Dragged all the way down the hallway
Where it found its home
Home in the (janitor's) closet

But it didn't hurt
For we have lived in closets before
For we have lived as trash

Such was the fitting reminder
That even if pride was a month
Straight is the year. A millennium. A lifetime
But it doesn't hurt
The closet has been home
And home has been trash

Dance With Me

Dance with me; in the dead of the night
For the dawns are what I dread

They used to help him shine afore
Now it burns my skin to the core
Perching my naked skin

So, dance with me; in the dead of the night
Hold me in your arms
Hold me tight

When the world is empty
And our hearts are full
Just you and me and our aching souls

Come, my beloved
The night that's dead
For the dawns are what I dread

Engineered World

Engineered lies believed to be facts
Engineered attacks believed to be spontaneous

Engineered stories believed to be NEWS
Engineered hope believed to be the future

Engineered love believed to be real

A mechanical world living a mechanical life
With the power to create anything

But all we engineer are hate, lies, and betrayal

What Happens To The Words You Never Say?

What happens to those words
From the depths of your heart?
Those words you never say
Not even to yourself

Do they leech you from within
And make your souls hollow?
Or do they soak & sink you?
Making it heavier every day?

What stops you from saying them?
Is it the fear of souring the relationship
Or of losing them altogether?

Would you have said it to them
If there were no consequences?
Or would you continue to suffer?

You can hide it from the world
You can hide from the world
But how do you hide from yourself?

Floodgates

There it breaks
The floodgate of his sanity

There it comes
The surge of her worst fears
His insecurities, his failures

Washing down the remains
Of his dead spirit
And everything he once believed
Everything he once dreamt of

There he stands
In the middle of it, once again

Not screaming for help
Not trying to stay afloat

But keeping his arms wide open
Waiting to embrace this bloody mess
The one he created himself

Just Tell Her You Love Her

Smack her hard in the face and let her weep in
your arms.
Kiss her swollen lips.
Touch her quivering body turned black and blue.
Make her feel warm in the same arms that made
her tremble.

Tell her you love her.
With the same lips.
That spoke of killing her moments ago.

She thought her time was up. That she'd be gone
in today.
But she will survive. One more night.

In your bed. In your arms. With your warmth.
Weeping in your arms.
Kissing with her swollen lips.
Embracing with her bruised body.
Her broken bone. Her broken soul.

She will survive. One more night.
If you just tell her you love her.

Screw You Pandora

And that night, she cried a million tears
And died a million deaths

When all she needed was one
The one that took courage
That one that would end it all

The one that didn't happen
Because hope still lingered on

The hope that this will end
Not life but the suffering
Give yourself one more day, she'd say

And days become weeks
Weeks become months
You know how that goes

Screw you, Pandora
You had one job
You shouldn't have opened that box
Or should have let it all out

And so she cries a million tears
And she dies a million deaths
Even as that hopeless hope lingers on

The next day she wakes up
With eyes red and swollen
Pretending as if nothing is going on
Everything is fine, everything is routine

But as the day passes by
The toxins seep in
The mind becomes a leper
And heart a frozen bone

What can one do
To a sedated mind?
And a heart comatose?

So, that night again
she cries a million tears
And dies a million deaths

Except for the one
That could simply end it all

Fragile

Isn't it strange how we assume?
That everything is in our control
That everything is and can be planned

All until one day
The reality tears it apart
Like a hot air balloon on fire
You can't stop it. You can't save it
All you do is watch it drift away into nothingness

Like the sand that slips away from your hand
Like a broken piece of mirror
The harder you hold it
The smaller pieces it breaks into

And even if you put the pieces together
What are you going to do about the cracks?
Those cracks would always be a reminder
Of your broken past

That's how fragile this life is
All you can say is, "Who would have thought?"
And then move on
Move on with the scars from that broken glass

To Harun Nair, his family, and friends

Shadows

Do our shadows sit around
and laugh at us when we sleep
At our follies and insecurities?

Or do they just weep
In a corner, while we look away
And pretend to laugh happily?

I Killed A Bird

I killed a bird one day
With a poison called hate
And a harpoon called doubt

But that's not it
There was some isolation too
Until it was strangled by its own veins

Watched it grow pale
Stared into its eyes
Wondered why it did not cry

Could it have called for help?
Would someone come?
Or would I scare them away?

Perhaps it is too late to say
--
I killed myself one day
With poison called hate
And a harpoon called doubt

But that's not it
There was some isolation too
Until I was strangled by my own veins

Watched myself grow pale
Looked at me
Wondering why I did not cry

Could I have called for help?
Would someone come?
Or would I push them away,
Just to let myself die?

Perhaps it is too late to say
——-

Did I kill the bird?
Or was it dead when I got there?
Can you kill a bird that's already dead?

Let's End It

"If you don't end yourself, I will"
"Who are you?"

"I am YOU"

"There is no way out, is there?"
"Do you want a way out?"
"Maybe this is the way out"

"All right then. Let's end it"
"Let's end it"

Ocean

How far do you walk into the ocean
Till you reach nowhere
And see nothing around you?

To the point of no return

To the point where
You can do nothing
But wait to be consumed by it

And vanish forever.

Phone Line

22

How often do you stare at your phone
Waiting to hear from someone?

Do you itch to pick up that phone
And reach out to them?

What prevents you?
As you wonder what prevents them

Is it that deep down, you know
That the lines are clear
But the connection is lost? Forever.